Slow Air

by the same author

A PAINTED FIELD

ROBIN ROBERTSON

Slow Air

HARCOURT, INC.

Orlando ⋆ Austin ⋆ New York ⋆ San Diego ⋆ Toronto ⋆ London

Requests for permission to make copies of any part of the work
should be mailed to the following address:
Permissions Department, Harcourt, Inc., 6277 Sea Harbor Drive,
Orlando, Florida 32887-6777.

www.HarcourtBooks.com

Library of Congress Cataloging-in-Publication Data
Robertson, Robin, 1955–
Slow air / Robin Robertson.—1st U.S. ed.
p. cm.
ISBN 0-15-100746-2
I. Title.
PR6068.O1925 S58 2003
823'.914—dc21 2002038934

First published in the UK by Picador

Text set in Dante
Designed by Scott Piehl

Printed in the United States of America
First U.S. edition
A C E G I H F D B

in memory of my father

vanitas vanitatum, et omnia vanitas

Ecclesiastes

and the fruit of my vanity is shame,
and repentance, and the clear knowledge
that whatever the world finds pleasing,
is but a brief dream

Petrarch

CONTENTS

ACKNOWLEDGMENTS

Agenda, Arts Council Awards Anthology, Boston Review, DoubleTake, Dream State (Polygon), *Dublin Review, The Fiddlehead, Flora Poetica* (Chatto & Windus), *Guardian, Independent, Last Words* (Picador), *London Review of Books, Love for Love* (Morning Star/Polygon), *Meanjin, New Statesman, New Writing 9* (Vintage), *New York Review of Books, New Yorker, Observer, Paris Review, Penguin Book of the Sonnet* (Penguin), *Penguin Modern Poets 13* (Penguin), *Ploughshares, Poetry, Poetry Wales, Sunday Times, Tabla Book of New Verse 1998, Thumbscrew, Times Literary Supplement, Verse.*

The writing of this has been greatly assisted by an Arts Council Writer's Award, grants from the Author's Foundation and the Artist Fund of the New York Foundation for the Arts, and by time spent in the Tyrone Guthrie Centre at Annaghmakerrig.

My grateful thanks go to the editors—Alice Quinn, Ben Sonnenberg, Jean Stein and Drenka Willen in New York, and John Lanchester, Jean McNicol, Andy O'Hagan and Don Paterson in London and Edinburgh—for their advice, support and hospitality.

Slow Air

APART

We are drawn to edges, to our own
parapets and sea-walls: finding our lives
in relief, in some forked storm.

Returning with our unimaginable gifts,
badged with salt and blood,
we have forgotten how to walk.

Thinking how much more we wanted
when what we had was all there was;

looking too late to the ones we loved,
we stretch out our hands as we fall.

HEAD OVER HEELS

for Clare

Holding hands on the big wheel
ninety feet above the Tuileries'
evening jasmine, I loved
your play at fear,
my brave stab at insouciance,
the way the bright circuitry of Paris
lay beneath us like the night sky,
like the plan of our lives.

HOLD SLIP

Pickup library: WHIPPANY
Item ID: 0101201137607
Title: ILL--WIP--001
User name: Whippanong
ILL user ID
User ID: ILL-WIP

HOLD SLIP

WEDDING THE LOCKSMITH'S DAUGHTER

The slow-grained slide to embed the blade
of the key is a sheathing,
a gliding on graphite, pushing inside
to find the ribs of the lock.

Sunk home, the true key slots to its matrix;
geared, tight-fitting, they turn
together, shooting the spring-lock,
throwing the bolt. Dactyls, iambics—

the clinch of words—the hidden couplings
in the cased machine. A chime of sound
on sound: the way the sung note snibs on meaning

and holds. The lines engage and marry now,
their bells are keeping time;
the church doors close and open underground.

THE LANGUAGE OF BIRDS

The sides of the hill
are stubbed with fire-pits.
The sky is paraffin blue.

A pigeon's heart swings here
on the kissing-gate, withered,
stuck through with pins,

while out on the estuary,
beaks of birds needle
to the wind's compass,

the sky's protocol.
Swans go singing out to sea,
the weather is changing cold.

     *

In the elm above me, a magpie chuckles
and turns the magic wand of itself
away, towards the light.

I climb to the seeing rock
high over the pines; a blown squall
of rooks rises and settles like ash.

I saw the hay marry the fire
and the fire walk.
The sky went the colour of stone.

The cattle sickened:
what milk that came
came threaded, red as dawn.

    *

Down below, in the grey fall
of heather and gorse,
a swithering flame.

Hooded crows haunt the highway,
pulling at roadkill;
their heads swivel to watch.

I've seen them murder their own,
the weak or the rare, those
with the gift of tongues.

I keep an albino one in a box.
I can't let go of it
till it tells me its name.

MAROON, OVER BLACK ON RED

Threshold

In the fall of '58
at the Whitney,
trying to escape
a hated critic,
he missed the doorway
and put both hands
through the plate glass:
an after-image
of the black grave,
forecast in red.

Maroon

This is the light
through closed eyes:
the dark corona
fraying the edges
of the slammed door;
turbulence playing
in the face of it all—
the black ingots made
from absence, the red
drawn from life.

Art Lesson

She stood at his
burnt windows
until she saw herself
answered in their dark,
the way glass gets
blacked at night
in a lighted room.
She went home,
pulled the curtains;
drew a red bath.

Exit

On the wall of the studio
on East 69th
his last canvas: a large,
unfinished study in reds.
On the floor: exsanguination
via the brachial artery;
six foot by eight;
black on red; unframed.
Signed by the artist
in the crook of his arm.

NIGHTDRIVING

Straight on through the rifled dark,
the headlights film the road:

light pools ahead as the land dips—
the skid and slur of sodium

hangs, traced in the eyes,
as the road reels in to the sound

of sirens, crowding the night.
The cars in front are slowing down.

THE OVEN MAN

for Colin Greenwood & Molly McGrann

The house re-inflates
its skin of heat:

tightens it up
to the screen door,

frames creaking
like a boat at anchor.

The burners cut out
before the roof lifts.

The house rustles
and ticks, and clicks off.

During all this commotion
I am inside, in expansive mood,

relaxing
like a Sunday roast

in my juices,
my puddle of blood.

MARCH, LEWISBORO

for Shelby White & Leon Levy

The estate at dawn hangs
like smoke; the forest

drawn in grainy bands
of smeared, cross-hatched,

illegible trees: a botched
photocopy of itself.

Swamp maple, sugar maple,
red and white oak; first light lifts

the pale yellow flare
of a beech tree's papery leaves.

Where are you going?
What on earth's the time?

A salting of snow, blown
across the white table of the lake:

thrown leaves scrape and scratch
the hard new surface,

to be fluked away,
in another gust, like cards.

What life there is is felt and phantom:
limbs lost under the locking ice,

glimpsed, half-heard beginnings;
the vestiges, and signs.

Turn off the light! Please,
I'm trying to get some sleep.

The oiled rook strides
into the wind's current,

ransacks some twigs, then
opens herself into the air;

ducks, flummoxed, slither
and skite on the ice.

Run me a bath when you get back,
I'm freezing here.

The love-blind swan climbs out,
head crooked, neck folded flat,

to drag-walk and
swagger after the Canada goose.

His mate nests on the island;
will watch all this for months.

What's wrong with you
that you can never sleep?

In the sky, five crows
are bringing down a hawk—

their cries are lost
and he is lost,

among the pines, far out
over the reservoir.

The frost's acoustic
futile against such silence:

a dog's bark, like a gun,
just ricochets.

And if you're going to the store
you better get me my magazine.

Stations of the necessary dead:
the drenched mop of rabbit,

its eyes (which would have dimmed
like the drying of ink) not present;

the crow's umbrella spokes
abandoned in a pool of stress.

The soil's peristalsis
gives up baseballs, glass bottles,

its usual spoil of stone
eased to the surface

only to be erased again
by another fall;

the slub in the immaculate lawn
is the missing roe deer,

her warm wounds hung
in their sheaths of snow.

Why don't you come back to bed?
You can walk any time.

Wind breathes life into leaves
till the trees are speaking,

and under a sudden, exorbitant
flush of light,

a spruce stands
thickly green and lucent

over tiny arrows in the snow
pointing, unmistakably, to the junco

and the chickadee, flickers,
grosbeaks, a white-winged crossbill—

the feeder is ribboned with goldfinches,
sapsuckers: a maypole of birds.

Squirrels bicker underneath
in the spill of millet.

Do what you want.
You always do anyway.

On the slopes, daffodils begin to show
the green of their bills;

flower varieties, painted on sticks,
people the hollows:

Manon Lescaut is here,
and Jules Verne,

Rip Van Winkle bedded down
with Salome and Rosy Splendour;

Burning Heart, Martinette,
Gigantic Star.

And check the mail!
I'm expecting a letter.

Behind the house, stone sphinxes
and a line of statues, trussed up,

black-bagged for the frost:
like hostages

or the already cold and
unnegotiable dead.

Have you gone already?
I was talking to you.

White-tails have leapt an eight-foot fence
to crop the rhododendrons;

one by one
they raise their heads to stare

—stage-struck—then jink away,
amazed, back

into their element,
which is breath.

The sun has cleared the trees
but gives out

nothing now but glare.
All the colours are too bright:

the chemical red of a cardinal;
the forsythia's astringent

yellow gold; stars of glass
on the drive; all these radiant

cars and houses;
the speeding road.

My grey notebook.
This glossy magazine and mail.

HANGING FIRE

The impatience for summer
is desire: ritual, imbedded
hard as a hinge
in the earth's mesh.
From the papery bulb,
the spurred, flesh-green horn
pushes, straining for air—
flexes its distended,
perfect, cleft muscle
out and up through the crust.

Then the deeper sleep of August,
ninety degrees of hanging fire:
the yellow lawns, the blighted
flowerless trees, the malformed leaves
sticky with sarcoma; the only sound
the hot tick of tarmac.
The pigeon splays
and struts, drags his thickening tail
behind him through the dust.

Once it comes
we want it over: the rain
to wash it all away,
and frosts to kill it back—
to start again next spring
with that familiar pulse,
that stirring of old ground:
that ache we think is lust.

MARYCULTER, 1972

I wanted to become a man
badly, like him. He used to say,
'That's the trouble with women:
all they think about is love.'

Later that summer, in a field,
the cone of flies attendant
on my first liquefaction
told me three things:
that sex is death;
that life is not drawn,
but traced; and that
all theft is the theft of love.

BREAK

Washing glasses in the sink
and the first thing she knew was this
dull click, like a tongue,
under the soap-suds.
The foam pinked.
Now she could see blood
smoking from the flap of skin,
and it was over, clearly,
out in the open:
holding water, feeling nothing.

RAISING THE PAINT

Pleased by the ruined bed,
the full ashtray,
I checked my glass for finger-marks,
turning it, over and over.
As I left the house
I ran the key
along the panels of the door,
raising the paint.
The tide was out,
and each step whitened the sand
like pressed skin.
Behind me, all this evidence:
an almost straight line
of footprints,
clothes, credit cards,
proving I exist.

TRYST

The sunset's slow catastrophe of reds
and bruised blues
leaches the land to its green and grey.
Light thins over the wood; black
colours—in each notch and furrow
at the long day's closing-down.
The only sounds are bled,
and far away:
the cough of an axe
and the lowing roar of distant chainsaws
starting and falling, like cattle
calling out to be milked.
And so I wait here, as usual,
in the crushed silence of tinder: steeped,
stepped in shadow,
under the appalling pines.

EXPOSURE

Rain, you said, *is silence turned up high.*
It has been raining now for days.
Even when it stops
there is still the sound
of rainwater, labouring
to find some way into the ground.

We lie in grim embrace: these
two halves trying to be whole, straining
for this break in the static,
in the white noise
that was rain falling
all day and all through the sheeted night.

Silence is rain with the sound turned down,
and I stare out now on a clear view
of something left out on the line:
a life, snagged there—
drenched, shrunken,
unrecognisably mine.

THE HARBOUR WIFE

The steady-burning pilot's light
rides out, and is gone in the gale.
There is fear behind her eyes

as she turns, goes inside
to her tea, to the heat of the range:
its steady-burning pilot light

her only light, now she is blind
in the dark from the tears in her face,
that fear behind the eyes.

Years spent waiting; waiting spent. The night's
flare of matches, the coaxed flame,
the steady-burning pilot light
of fear behind the eyes.

FALSE SPRING

A lift in the weather: a clemency
I cling to like the legend

of myself: self-exiled,
world-wounded, god

of evenings like this,
eighty degrees and half a world away.

    *

All night, the industry
of erasure, effacement,

our one mouth
working itself dry.

    *

But even a god can't stop the light
that finds us, annealed,

fruitless, two strangers
broken on the field of day.

In the window-box,
the narcissi come up blind.

THE WOOD OF THE SUICIDES

after Dante (Inferno, Canto XIII)

Beyond the barking of the damned in the red river, before the phosphorus sand: another dark wood. A tangle of thorn and bitter leaves, torn at by women with the feet of birds; perched there in the barren trees they dismember and defile.

A descant rises under their shrieks and the batter of wings: a low, encroaching moan of grief. The groans of millions fill the ruined wood.

Two men have come amongst us:
sight-seers; voyeurs. One takes
the twig of my finger in his hand
and snaps the bone.
The pain is sudden, and remote.
I am run through by flame.
The stump starts to sweat and sputter,
like a green reed half-in,
half-out of the fire,
one end burning, the other bubbling
air and sap and blood, whistling,
spitting out
words:

'You know now what I am.
                    Like you, poet,
I was expelled from my own land; but unlike you
I could look no longer on what I saw

and killed what hurt me.
I closed my own eyes.
And for this crime
I was banished from my body;
it lies in the upper ground
while my soul was tossed like a seed
into this deep hole, and has grown to a tree.
                    Like you, poet,
these creatures come
to rest in my limed branches,
destroying them:
giving pain, and giving pain a voice.

They say that on the final day
I can claim my skin,
but being self-killed
can never wear it.
I will drag it down here
—as the butcher-bird—
and skewer my body
on my soul's thorn.

You have heard my story and can leave,
as you leave all the lost.
I made my home my hanging-tree.
Now let me drop.'

ANXIETY #2

Leaving the building in a hurry, I find myself on the edge of a wide and empty urban square. Behind me, frightened people gather in the doorway. Looking into the centre of the square where the streets intersect, there is something long and white, slowly revolving. As I walk closer I see it is a 20-foot bone, one end still carrying shreds of matter, turning on its own axis—as if something huge had just passed by, and nudged it, accidentally.

A commotion further on, and I see beasts—hyenas perhaps— tearing at something enormous and unrecognisable.

ANXIETY #3

Returning to my uneaten meal, everything has gone cold. My host—a member of the club—suggests he takes advantage of his private walk-in fridge so that we might sample the rare meat selection, freshly stocked each day. He comes back with a large white plastic box and passes it to me. Prising back the lid, I see various anonymous greased-proof-paper packages, some cellophaned steaks—and, in the corner, something pink and agitated, suddenly joined by a twin. My host looks me in the eye and says: dormice—ready-shaved for the pot.

ANXIETY #5

I need to go to the bathroom. Inside it is very bright, with spotless white tiles from floor to ceiling. As I am washing my hands, I notice the door of the shower is covered in pieces of coloured paper. Crossing the room, I see that these are Polaroids, taped neatly in rows. They show a man going through the stages of torture with a razor blade, his mouth held shut with the same duct-tape used to display the photographs; the interior, visible behind him, clearly the same bathroom.

The process had been drawn out over some time: a number of the wounds had already congealed. The lines were very straight—across the face and chest, around the arms, and so on—like the lines on graph-paper. In the first photo you can see his eyes. By the end he is unrecognisable. The last photograph is blurred.

There is no sign of blood on the white tiles; they are clean and fresh. I return to the Polaroids and notice the last one is not blurred anymore, it is still developing. I begin to make out the back of a man's head. He is looking at pieces of coloured paper.

THE LARCHES OF ZERNIKOW

These lines of larch were planted
by children, here among the pines
and firs in 1938, they think, or '39.
Even if you walked beneath them now
in October, you would never know
that for these two weeks
the yellow gold of these hundred trees
would be branding the forest canopy
far above you,
blazing a swastika
you could see from the moon.

FROM THE JARDIN DES PLANTES

after Rilke

The Panther

Exhausted, he sees nothing now but the bars
that flicker past him in a blur;
it seems there are a thousand bars
and behind the thousand bars an empty world.

The drill of wheel and return: turning on his heel till
he seems to pass through his own body—like whisky
swilled to the neck of the bottle then back on itself.
He swings on the pivot of his numb and baffled will.

Sometimes, though, the sprung shutter of the eyes
will slide open and let an image enter—a face, perhaps—
shooting through the tensed muscles, lightening
the limbs, streaming into his heart to die.

The Gazelle

Tranced creature: no rhyme or ringing words
can match the pulse that rolls
through you like a charm. Horns spring
from your head, adorning you with leaf and lyre,

and you are your own metaphor,
just as the words of a love-song
are like a drift of rose-petals, closing
the eyes of the tired reader, so as to see you—

there—hair-triggered,
four legs pointed, ready
to recoil and ricochet away

but waiting, listening: just as
the bathing huntress heard the forest stir,
and turned, the quivering pool reflected in her face.

The Flamingos

Fragonard and his looking-glass worlds
could no more capture this red and white
than words can conjure the flesh of a lover:
so tender, soft and full of sleep . . .

They rise through green beds on their high pink stems,
swaying gently in full bloom: mesmeric,
self-mesmerised, till the scooped heads sink
and bury those white-rimmed eyes
with the other colours: black and red wing-
feathers hidden in their feathery sides.

A jealous screech shivers through the aviary
like shattering glass. They spread their wings,
surprised, and one by one, each stretches, slowly,
and stalks away: striding into paradise.

ITAMAI-SAN

for James Lasdun

Sashimi

Watching the hands' transaction
at the deal table, it is hard to tell:

does the knife swipe through mackerel
clean as a credit card,

or is it the silver fish itself
that swipes the blade?

His raw hands cut the deck.
The flesh is dealt.

Sushi

Onto the squeezed
fistfuls of rice

dabbed with wasabi
he presses

a slice of tuna,
cuttlefish, yellowtail;

shapes each one
into a thumb.

THE THERMAL IMAGE

The side of the house came away
like a glacier calving,
opening up four floors
in a suck of vertigo:
staircases walking nowhere,
doors going into the air—
the bedroom wallpaper
now clashing with the lawn,
the full-length mirror
mirroring the sky.

The shell is broken
and the building's heat is streaming out;
my camera sees it as a white cloud.
I pick up residuals from the wiring
and the hearth, faint glows
from a sofa and the fogged-up
roll-top bath. It's like cracking open
logs to find fireflies.

I move around the city
looking for the hotspots:
the heat signatures of love,
of too much blood;
one hundred watts at rest, rising
to a thousand *in extremis*.
Blackbodies, glow-worms,
ghosts of radiation:

I track and root out heat,
its absorption and emission,
the white bed's infra-red, the bright
spoor of the soul's transmission.

DREAM OF THE HUNTRESS

It is always the same:
she is standing over me

in the forest clearing,
a dab of blood on her cheek

from a rabbit or a deer.
I am aware of nothing

but my mutinous flesh,
and the traps of desire

sent to test it—
her bare arms, bare

shoulders, her loosened hair,
the hard, high breasts,

and under a belt
of knives and fish-lures,

her undressed wound.
Every night the same:

the slashed fetlock,
the buckling under;

I wake in her body
broken, like a gun.

VANITY SONG

What shall I bring you
now that you've gone?
Cutworm, gall-fly and codling moth.

What will I sing now
instead of a song?
The cry of a gull and the curlew's call.

What can I make you
for breaking this bond?
I will make you remember the emptying night,

and the shame will be your reward.

ASTERION AND THE GOD

nec enim praesentior illo est deus

Asterion, his name is, King of Stars.
Some joke of his father's, who now
stables him here in these spiralled halls,
this walled-up palace, where shame
cries itself to sleep.

Where is my mother? Why
has she left me here alone?
This is a house of many corners
but only one room, made of stone.
I live inside this stone.

See how he prowls and paces,
my beast of a boy; moving round
his world, looking at his emptiness
from new directions.
He will have a visitor soon.

Poor monster, pulling at himself,
the DNA unspooling from his hand:
white butterflies
spill into the dark.
Out of the broken comes forth brine.

Sometimes children visit, to dance here
and play leapfrog, singing loudly,
full of wine; but they break so easily
and then it is very quiet again.
Where did I lose my life?

Fretting all night at a red bone
he makes a mirror from the slick
and sees himself, at last, in the stone
of the running walls: lustral,
horned, bearded with blood.

I hear through the walls what I am,
what I do; sparagmos, *they call it,*
whatever that is.
They say a stranger comes
to release me. Let him come soon.

She pledged herself to me, but now
carries the crown I gave her
to light the stranger's way. The hero
who has come to kill Asterion:
her half-brother, my son. My self.

They betray each other so perfectly:
husband to wife, wife to husband;
sister to half-brother, and now
lover to lover. The symmetries
of chaos and bliss. The mysteries.

I am the true vine,
I am the fennel stalk;
and he will be honey:
buried to the horns, his body
home to the bee-swarm.

She has gone, now, with her hero,
who is already forgetting her.
I, however, never forget. She will hang
in the night sky like a princess
from a clew of twine.

Sometimes we speak, sometimes
we let the gods speak through us.
I am half; he is twice-born.
My grief still here
and I am gone.

Imagine me as the wind—the force
animals and birds know
is there, but does not threaten:
part of their world, but other.
The god who comes; the god who disappears.

AT KAIKOURA

I have driven through the mountains
in a turquoise jeep, to eat here
under these hills that come down to the sea:
a bowl of green-lipped mussels, each
exactly the size of my own mouth,
two local crayfish and a bottle
of cold South Island wine.
There are dolphins in the bay
and sperm whales out beyond the shelf,
trawling for squid. The sun is folded
into the water. I am far from home,
remembering how to live, remembering
I have no home.

THESE DAYS

The vessel he has carried for so long
is spilt;
his eyes have run out of light, and are
looking beyond us to the far distances,
the simplicities.
My own eyes star.

His great priest's face
taking on a cast,
becoming immemorial, a man
becoming something else:
a ruined shell, a wasted king
amongst the debris, a mask.

The slow shutting down of the machine
till it felt like hours between each breath,
trawled, heaved up,
each from a greater depth.
We listen to his heartbeat's muffled drum
until the drumming stops.

A poor likeness. Pen-and-ink. Not him
at all. We are mourners sketched
at the death-bed, in a *trompe l'œil*
of personal effects: his toilet bag and shoes,
his watch, his cigarettes; and the drawn skull
of my father, dispersed.

Waking up the next morning into a wet
brightness and hugeness of day,
the miniature figures
going to work, and the world around them,
carrying on.
I can hardly walk, I am so frightened.

These days are scored through, one by one.
The ward-plan wiped clean for another name;
another man lies in the bed behind the glass.
My mother struggles with the singular.
We all must learn to use another tense:
the past.

UNDERGROUND

At the very edge of the train's torrent,
its horizontal through-fall, you can feel it
clearing the platform's length like a piston
of grey and grey and grey,
pushing air in front of it,
pulling it behind; gone
leaving less than nothing, just that faint
pitch forward
into its pocket of loss.

DEAD SHEEP IN CO. DERRY

In a scatter of wool and its own litter
the skull stares out at the road below: socket rings
cool as trigger-guards. The furled-paper sinuses
fragile under the muzzle's tuning-fork;
the four plates of the face with their scribbled fissures:
the crazed cruciform of the frontier marks
keeping white from white, nothing from nothing.
She hefts it, turns the bone on its own orbit.
Returning its gaze, she fingers the unmanned interior,
the smooth sides. Lobs it into a ditch.

THE LONG HOME

I hadn't been back in twenty years
and he was still here, by the fire,
at the far end of the longest bar-counter
in Aberdeen—some say Scotland.
Not many in, and my favourite time:
the dog-watch; the city still working,
its tortoiseshell light just legible
in the smoked windows,
and through the slow delay of glass
the streetlights
batting into life.

The firewood's sap
buzzing like a trapped fly,
the granular crackle of a *Green Final*
folded and unfolded,
the sound of the coals
unwrapping themselves like sweets.
He only looked up when the barman
poured a bucketful of ice
into the sink, like a tremendous
burst of applause.

He was drinking Sweetheart Stout
and whisky, staring into the glass
of malt as if it were the past, occasionally
taking a pull on the long brown bottle.
I remember him telling me,
with that grim smile,

'I'm washing my wounds in alcohol.'
I liked a drink too,
but would always leave before him,
walking home, as if on a wire.

I'd heard what had happened
but wasn't ready for the terrible wig,
all down at one side, the turn
in his mouth and his face's
hectic blaze. He'd left here so bad
he could barely stand.
He'd got through his door, back to his room
and passed out for the night,
sleeping like a log with his head in the fire.

WAKING LATE

I am used to the smell by now,
the stillness, these shifts
in waist measurement,
the bad skin. But my hair
is lustrous, the cheekbones
well-defined, and my nails,
it seems, still growing.

DEAD WOOD

for Tom Lynch

Huge glossy beetles
doze in this room,
each with a lifted wing-case
the size of a car door.
They are only fed once,
then close themselves
with a click.
Too heavy to fly
in their mahogany and oak,
they have grown handles.

BALSAM LAKE, ONTARIO

for Scott & Krystyne Griffin

1.
Sussex, at twenty,
twenty years ago:

resinous, *quick-in-hand*,
impatient by the river bank,

one trailing fingernail
would trigger the seedhead.

2.
September now, and dusk:
this lake so still

under the wafered moon
it makes a stern geometry

from the stems: chevrons and lozenges
of the wounded *touch-me-not*.

MAKING THE GREEN ONE RED

The Virginia creeper has built its church here
in the apple tree: vermilion
lacework, pennons, tendrils
of scarlet and amber,
hung through the host like veins.
Spangled and jaspered, shot with red,
the tree filled with sun is stained glass:
a cathedral of blood and gold.

It took me years to find the creeper's roots,
knotted in a mulch of leaves and the fallen,
forgotten fruit: the arms espaliered
like Christ to the garden wall. Its red
has reached this first-floor window now,
the apple tree is dead.

SORROWS

An over-filled glass:
I take my head
in my hands,
careful not to spill.

    *

Without a real death in my life
I had to make my own.

Now I build models of my father
out of smoke and light.

    *

He was uncomfortable,
so I asked the nurse
if we could lift him higher.
He died an hour later.
Usually happens, she explained,
after you move them.
Forgive me, I say, at his feet,
through a mouthful of nails.

    *

In his shirt-sleeves and flannels
I remember him:

a stitch in his side
from the long run home.

★

The dam he built
in the stream is finally broken:
cold Highland water
rushing to the sea.

WAVES

I have swum too far
out of my depth
and the sun has gone;

the hung weight of my legs
a plumb-line,
my fingers raw, my arms lead;

the currents pull like weed
and I am very tired
and cold, and moving out to sea.

The beach is still bright.
The children I never had
run to the edge

and back to their beautiful mother
who smiles at them, looks up
from her magazine, and waves.

TO THE ISLAND

The fog rolling in towards San Michele
is folding round and over the lampposts
that are all that remain of some drowned street
and now guide the vaporetti
and the funeral barge with its black plumes
across the lagoon in a shawl of rain
to the cypresses of San Michele.

CURVE

for Karl Miller

Under the mouth
of the moon: a bank

of snow-gloved gorse,
and far below, the sea,

wrecking itself
against the rocks.

In the flickering room
the fire

finds the whisky, lit
in its gold slot,

in the warm
heel of the glass.

A curve
of stone and wood,

things made
more beautiful by use;

the owl's snow-
fall flight,

the turning
pages of a book.

HIDE

I have been waiting for the black deer
all my life, hidden here in the dark
corner of the wood.
I see glimpses of them, breaking cover,
swinging away
to erase themselves in the deep trees.

They are implicit there, and will move
only if I hold still.
Though in a dream I have
they stand so near I can feel them breathing.
Then, when I look down,
I have disappeared.

Out at the wood's edge, the snorts
and coughs of the feeding herd.
A gust startles a lift of leaves, and they
scatter and bound like the far-off heads
of deer in the distance.
The wind drops and the trees are antlered.

FLUID

The integrity and tension
of the shoal
             shape-changing
but always

one whole thing
             like a swarm
or that net of birds
that moves
          unloosened
under bridges at dusk

to fish the insect-mist
that forms
         and unforms
above the mesh of shadows

there
       where the water
tightens
black into silver
          feeding
thickening to light

NATURAL HISTORY

after Pliny

Draw the curtain that
cannot be pulled, watch birds peck
at a painted field.

FALL

after Rilke

The leaves are falling, falling from trees
in dying gardens far above us; as if their slow
free-fall was the sky declining.

And tonight, this heavy earth is falling away
from all the other stars, drawing into silence.

We are all falling now. My hand, my heart,
stall and drift in darkness, see-sawing down.

And we still believe there is one who sifts and holds
the leaves, the lives, of all those softly falling.

NOTES

Wedding the Locksmith's Daughter
locksmith's daughter: 19th-century slang for a key.

The Language of Birds
a pigeon's heart . . . stuck through with pins: a charm sometimes used by lovesick or vengeful girls to summon or afflict their faithless lovers.

swans go singing out to sea: one of the more familiar legends about swans is that they sing before they die; Aristotle suggests that when they sense the approach of death the birds fly out to sea.

Maroon, Over Black on Red
Mark Rothko, 1903–1970. *The Legacy of Mark Rothko* by Lee Seldes (New York, 1978).

The Larches of Zernikow
A stand of Sudetan larch, 60 metres long by 60 metres wide, was planted in Zernikow, 100 kilometres north of Berlin, under the direction of forester Walter Schmidt as a tribute to the 1000-year Reich. Known locally as the *Hakenkreuzschonung*—the Swastika Plantation—it was not discovered until 1992 after an aerial survey of the region. The trees were felled, but the stumps could not be removed.

Asterion and the God
Asterion: the given name of the Minotaur, half-brother to Ariadne—the princess who betrayed the god Dionysus for the hero, Theseus.

nec enim praesentior illo est deus: as Acoetes says of Dionysus in Ovid's *Metamorphoses* (3, 658–9): 'no god is nearer than him'.

The Long Home
the long home: the grave.

Balsam Lake, Ontario
impatiens noli-me-tangere: wild balsam, which propagates by means of seed capsules which, when ripe, explode at the slightest disturbance.

Making the Green One Red
'this my hand will rather the multitudinous seas incarnadine, making the green one red.' (*Macbeth*, II, ii, 62).

Natural History
'In a contest between Zeuxis and Parrhasius, Zeuxis produced so successful a representation of grapes that birds flew up to the stage-buildings where it was hung. Then Parrhasius produced such a successful *trompe l'oeil* of a curtain that Zeuxis, puffed up with pride at the judgement of the birds, asked that the curtain be drawn aside and the picture revealed. When he realised his mistake, with an unaffected modesty he conceded the prize, saying that whereas he had deceived birds, Parrhasius had deceived him, an artist.' Pliny, *Natural History*, xxxv, 65, translated by John F. Healy (London, 1991).

As E. H. Gombrich notes, in *Meditations on a Hobby Horse and Other Essays on the Theory of Art* (London, 1994), p.104, 'any painted still-life is *ipso facto* also a *vanitas*'.

Fall
Rilke wrote 'Herbst' ('Autumn') in Paris on 11 September, 1902.

823.914   Robertson, Robin,
Rob   1955-

      Slow air.

$23.00

DATE			

$ 23.00   5/03